Three Steps Home

Also by Charlie Mitchell:

Gifts from the Heart of the Storm

Three Steps Home

Written by

Charlie Mitchell

Illustrated by

Lucja Fratczak-Kay

All rights reserved; no part of this book may be reproduced, stored in a retrieval system, or transmitted, in any form or by any means, without the prior permission in writing from the publisher, nor be otherwise circulated in any form of binding or cover other than that in which it is published and without a similar condition including this condition being imposed on the subsequent purchaser.

First published in Great Britain in 2024 by Starseed Parenting

Copyright © 2024 by Charlie Mitchell
Illustrations copyright © 2024 Lucja Fratczak-Kay
Formatting by The Amethyst Angel

ISBN: 978-1-7397679-2-1

The right of Charlie Mitchell to be identified as the author of this work has been asserted in accordance with the Copyright, Designs and Patents Act 1998.

Nothing in this book is to be taken as professional medical advice and is the opinion and experience of the author or her clients. The author and publisher accept no liability for damage of any nature resulting directly or indirectly from the application or use of any information contained within this book. Any information acted upon from this book is at the reader's sole discretion and risk.

All publications and links mentioned are correct at the time of publication but may be subject to change.

First Edition

I dedicate this book to three incredible teachers
in my life.

One has shown me the wisdom of watching,
and the power of tenacity.

One has shown me the depths of human compassion
and power of connection.

One has shown me the magic of unconditional love
and power of joy.

They are my children and I am in awe every day that I
have the privilege of being their mother.

My life was two dimensional before they arrived. Since, I
have discovered dimensions I could never have imagined
in my wildest dreams.

I am eternally grateful for their presence in my life, and
for all I have learned as I journey with them.

Thank you Cory, Ali and Thomas - with love,

Charlie ♡

And much love and gratitude to Rufus and Otis
for touching my life more recently.

Before we Start

The intention of *Three Steps Home* is to help people to connect with themselves, connect with their inner child and to connect with the bigger picture, the universe or Great Spirit - however people wish to describe that.

No matter how bad things get, when we connect with fully with ourselves, we are in a better position to respond to what is going on. We can make better choices and we can find new approaches that we may not have been able to explore before.

When we use neuroscience to look at brain development, we find we need a few key questions to be answered positively in order for us to learn, grow and develop:

1. **Do I make sense? Do my thoughts and feelings and experiences fit with this situation?** It could be a family situation, relationship, work, community, cultural, or the global situation.

2. **Do I matter? Am I important? Am I valued?** By myself and others.

When we can answer yes to both of these questions, we have an opportunity to flourish, even when life is tough and throws us a lot of curve balls. However, we cannot do this work on our own. We have to be with others who truly see us, who witness our experiences and who validate what we are feeling.

The foundation of the work of *Three Steps Home* is to create a community of people who are interested in helping each other to answer these questions positively, so that we are all supported in our inner journey, which helps us to deal with difficult situations in our outer world.

Magic happens when our need to be witnessed is met. We can share this magic be seeing others. We can learn to empathise with others and learn to receive that empathy ourselves. This is how we break pattern, change our lives and change the lives of others we come into contact with.

To find out more and join our community please visit:
www.starseedparenting.org

Ideas for making this story your own

You'll find space on the pages, and even space within the pictures. Feel free to doodle, colour parts in and create pictures or symbols that are helpful on your journey.

What images are meaningful for you?

Cross words out and write the words you would like to read. You can make these words even more meaningful and healing for you by adding your own words.

What words would you like to read? There are some reflective questions at the end of the each section to help you with your healing journey.

Your thoughts and feelings

Free Online Resources:

Free online resources including
- Three Steps Home book
- Gifts from the Heart of the Storm book
- guided meditations
- healing journal
- emotional first aid course
- self-coaching activities

www.starseedparenting.org/giftsbook

Step One

Connecting with myself

Truth

There's a space, deep in my belly, where magic lives.
Expansive. Endless.
Stretches far beyond me,
And lives within us all.

It is where I come home to myself.
It's quiet and gentle and is pure love.
It can hold everything effortlessly.
Every emotion is present and nothing is 'too much'.

The deep grief of loss.
The bliss of pure love.
The anger. The injustice.
The frustration. The joy.
All is welcome.

I sit with this magic in my belly,
I give it space.
I am the space.
And in this moment,
All is well.

Sit with one hand on your heart and one your hand on your belly.
Breathe deeply.
What do you feel?
What do you notice?
Journal on what you experience.
Repeat regularly.

Home

I have been searching
For such a long time.
Looking for answers and feeling adrift,
Not knowing where to turn,
Trying to make decisions by committee.

What do they think? What would they do?
Can they see the blind spot I have been missing?
Yet the truth is they don't know,
And I've just gone round in a circle
Finding myself back at the start
I've been here the whole time.

I breathe...

Suddenly I see myself properly for the first time.
I'm not lost. I'm not out of place.
I'm not broken. I'm not an outcast.
I meet the fullness of me, in all my glory.
Here in this moment, I realise
It's all as it needs to be.

A feeling of peace melts me.
I relax gently, all the way down into my bones.
I breathe deeply, feeling the spaciousness of my body
Breath nourishing everywhere it touches.
I am home. Meeting integrity.
My body is finally my sanctuary and all is well.

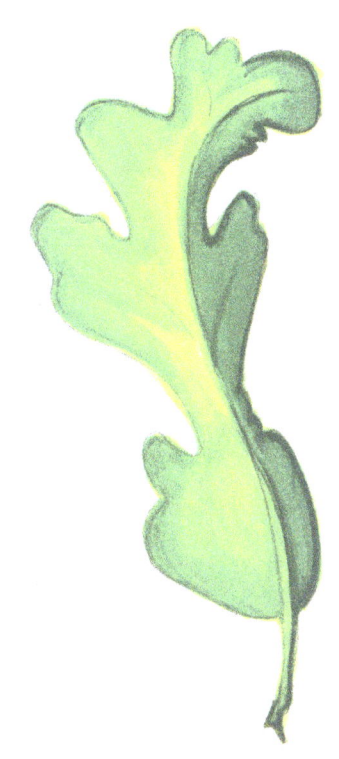

As you sit with one hand on your heart and one hand on your belly, breathe really deeply. Imagine your breath going back towards your spine and down deep into your hips.
Breathe out for longer than you breathe in.
Allow thoughts to float past.
Sit a little taller and fill your lungs a little deeper.
What do you notice?

Stories we tell Ourselves

I start to notice how things move me:
From deep peace, to chaos, into swirling confusion,
And back again.
As if I am ebbing and flowing like the ocean.
It is exhausting.
I wonder what will calm the waves?

I notice how my mind wanders from one thing...
to the next...
Sometimes with no rhyme or reason.
Yet the movement shifts my body's experience...
...from here to there....
I don't like getting caught up in these stories
That pull me into the drama, anxiety, and panic.

As I breathe slowly, I sink into presence
Here and now.
I notice how much goes on in my head:
Fear and judgement are rampant,
On the loose and out of control.
Peace runs for cover, hiding from the onslaught.

What meaning am I making of all this?
Am I the hero or the villain?
Victim or the perpetrator?
What if I step back from the story in my head?
What if I sink a little deeper into presence?
What is true?
What would love do?
Perhaps there is more here than just the story?

What are the common stories you tell yourself?
How do they make you feel?
Are they really true?
What if the opposite was true?
How would you like your story to be?
Experiment with your stories and
play with what feels good.
What do you notice?

The Spark

As I let go of the stories
There is some space for possibility.
I see how I make up the stories in my head,
They are just one perspective
Not the whole picture and they are not helpful.
I breathe deeply, feeling space
Expanding with new hope.

I glimpse another perspective
It's not just either this or that...
There are more options flowing in quick succession.
I smile as I feel open to what is emerging,
The magic of impossibility courses through my veins
Filling me with excited energy.

In this space a new view lands,
Different from what has been before.
Like the spark of a newly struck match
In the moment before the flame.
So much energy co-creating with the universe
As I make space and magic rushes in.

My body relaxes as I feel into this truth.
Life expands just a little today,
The world shifts in a whole new way,
The newness becomes real,
Melting into me as I breathe.
It becomes part of the here and now.

What does your spark mean to you?
Where do you notice it sits in your body?
Spend a moment connecting with your spark.
How does it feel?
Your spark has a message for you.
What does it want you to know?

Healing

In making space for this spark of an idea
There is more movement in the flow.
More than I realised or could have imagined.
In this space there is also a magical alchemy,
A moment when the manure transforms into pure gold
As I embrace my past and welcome all my feelings.

Nothing is off limits and nothing is rejected.
It is all welcome. Every moment. Every decision.
I listen for each and every mishap.
I make space and welcome my experiences home to me.
Loving each part. Even those parts...
Never spoken of or shamed into a dark corner.

At first it feels raw, and deeply exhausting.
Unconditional love melting into the deepest parts of me,
Finally bringing light to the heavy darkness.
I weep as I sink into the feelings
Still so sore, as if it happened yesterday,
When so many years have passed.

As the sobbing subsides, I notice
Peace is with me.
It is vaster, more solid somehow.
I feel into my toes and my feet
Noticing how I feel held by the universe
As my own roots reach a little deeper into the earth.

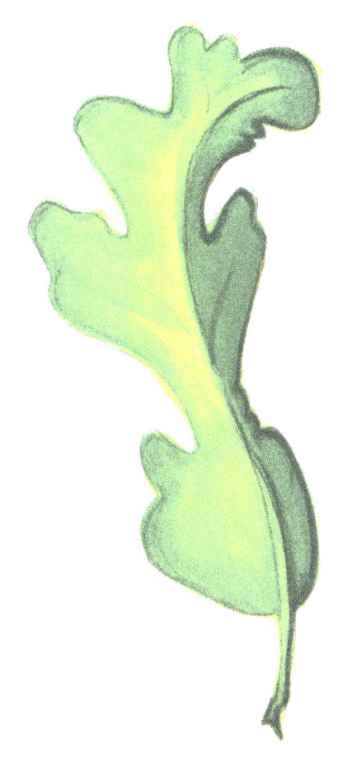

What do you love to embrace about your experiences?
What do you prefer to push away?
What do you need in order to connect
with these lost parts of yourself?
What would love say to you?
What supports your natural healing?

Creating Space for Me

I sit a little straighter and take up a little more space.
My shoulders lower as I relax,
I hold my head a little higher,
My heart expands.
A newness flows through me from head to foot
Like warm rays on a beautiful sunny day.

I give myself permission for all my experiences to be,
Here and now: this is freedom.
A smile dances across my lips,
My breath nourishing me from within
I create space for it all.
Every single decision, every action, every judgement.

Whatever I had thought about it
It's okay. I bring compassion.
I hold it gently with love,
Treating my experiences with dignity, respect and awe.
Even if I would make a different decision today
It's okay exactly as it is
Here is peace.

This is the unconditional love I searched for
Right here, right now.
I can love myself exactly as I am and give myself
The ultimate gift: accepting my own journey,
Bringing myself home,
And allowing all of my journey to be held lovingly.

What can you let go of to give yourself more space?
What can you do more slowly?
When are you most peaceful?
What does bringing yourself home mean to you?
What one action can you take today to
love yourself a little more?

Deep Empathy

Space for all of me feels like such a shift.
It feels so nourishing
Everything looks a little different.
Colours are sharper,
The birds sing a little sweeter
I notice love is all around me.

I start to notice the forks in the road,
The places where my life took a different turn.
The way I had judged myself,
And judged the people around me,
Making myself wrong for doing this or that
Or not doing the other.

Yet as I look back,
I realise that everything has led me here.
Nothing has been out of place
It has all been required.
I thought there were detours or things
that got in the way
Now I see it was all needed,
Every part of it a step on this journey.

Each challenge built my strength, my emotional muscles
Helped me to notice how much I am loved, held.
How many miracles cross my path each and every day.
Anything that still feels out of place is an
opportunity for love to grow
What would love do?
There are new opportunities at every turn.

Say to yourself:
I am here for you.
I love you.
I know things have been tough.
It makes sense you would feel like this.
I believe in you.
What else would you like to hear?
What else would help you feel loved?

Love

The more I notice the miracles, the more grateful I am
For the love that flows through my veins,
The people who go out of their way to help others,
The unexpected coincidences,
A stranger saying bless you when I sneeze,
The unseen people who built my house,
created my car, grew my breakfast.
'We are all held by a thousand hands',
the Indian saying goes and I feel it.

I also notice all the people who have
given their heart and soul,
Sometimes even their lives, so others can prosper.
The patterns of injustice that still continue,
fill my heart with grief.
What can I do to confront the wrongdoings?
I know there are opportunities
to bring love to every situation
Standing up for people who need our solidarity
to survive.

We can make a difference and bring love to life.
How can I bring more love to this situation?
I know my life is touched by love
and I can shine my light
So others' lives are brightened.
Every moment we can focus on love or fear.
We decide which one we allow to rest in our heart.

When we notice fear
We have an opportunity to choose love.
In that moment everything changes.
The shackles of the old patterns that held us back
Are broken.
We are released from our historic burdens
and are finally free.
We rise up with passion and take loving action
for the good of all.
Safe, secure and at peace, with love, and being loved.

What are you grateful for?
Who has inspired you in your life?
What can you do to support others?
How can you bring more love to this moment?
What helps you choose love?

Step Two

Connecting with my inner child

You are Safe

Darling one. Thank you for being in my life.
I have so much gratitude for you being here.
You are safe.
I am here to look after you,
To protect you and nurture you,
However things unfold.

There are many different people in the world
With many different ways of being.
I am here alongside you
Every step of the way.
I look around and notice the things
that could harm you or cause you pain.

I do what I can to keep those things at bay.
It doesn't always work and
Despite my best efforts,
There are still times
When your life is filled with pain.
I'm sorry you experience these challenges.

Yet challenge can help us to grow.
You know I am alongside you
and we take steps together.
You cry on my shoulder
and I hold you as you weep.
There is nothing you can say or do to stop me loving you
Or stop me being here when you need me.
Relax, my love, you are safe.

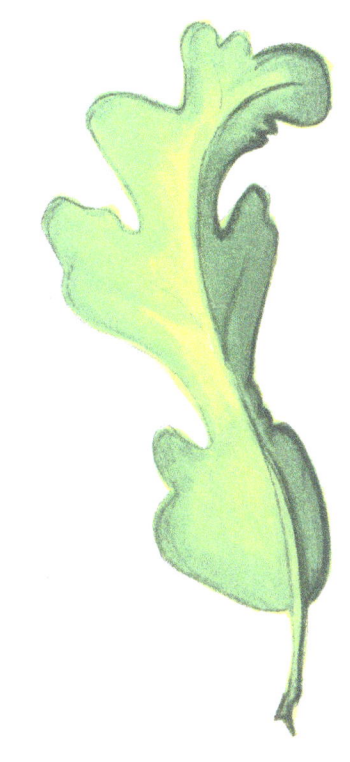

What helps you to feel safe?
Who are your safe people?
Spend some time with your inner child.
What do you notice?
How can you help your
inner child to feel safer?

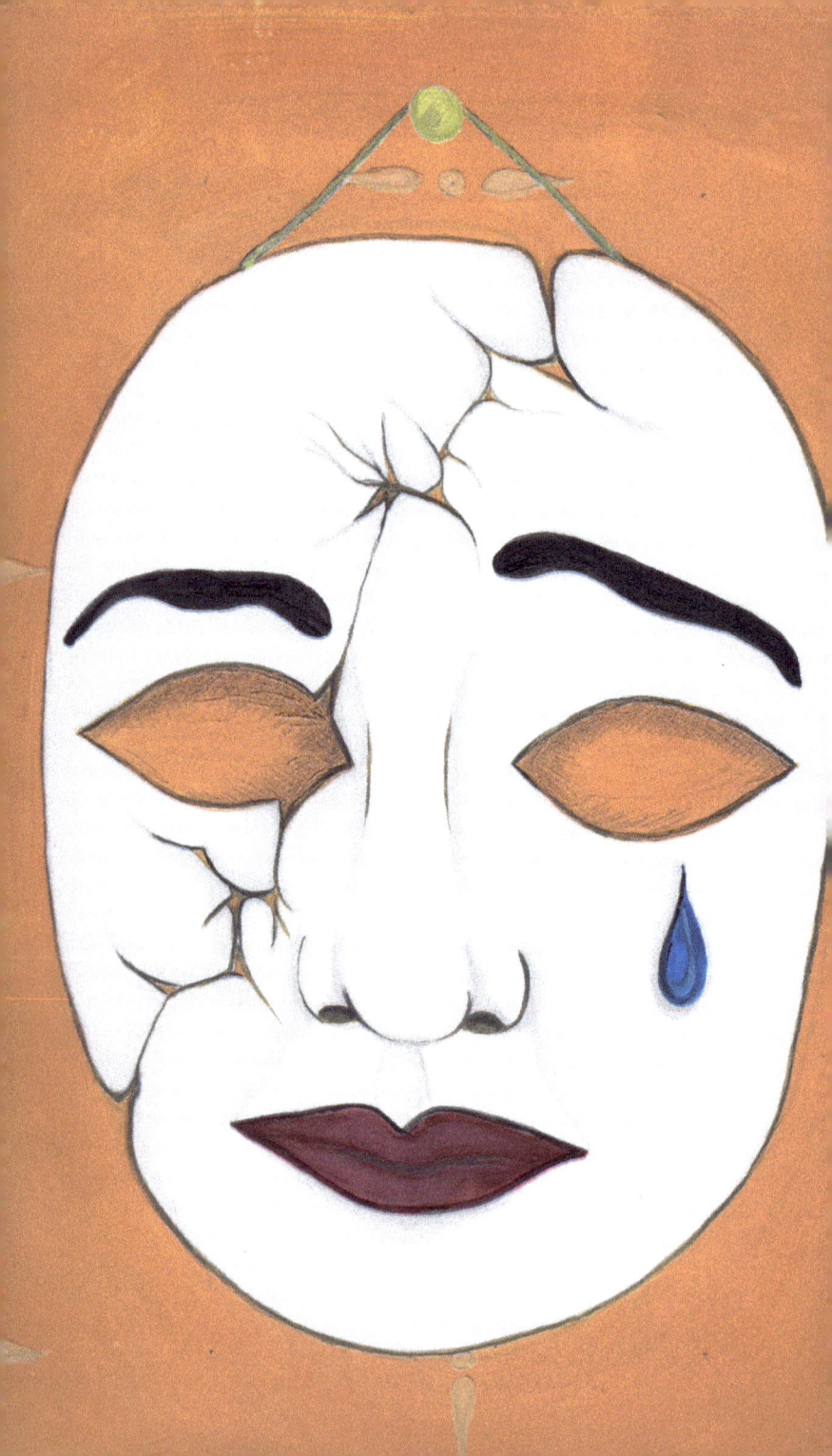

You Make Sense

It makes sense that you would have so many feelings,
The world turns upside down sometimes.
We can feel all kinds of emotions:
Fear, anger, sadness, joy, hope,
Grief, devastation, love and peace.
It's okay to feel these feelings.
All are welcome.

You don't need to hide any part of yourself.
It makes sense that you would have these feelings
in an uncertain world.
Sometimes the world feels harsh for us sensitive souls.
I am here for you, alongside you.
I can see how hard you try.
I see the effort you put in.
It's all okay.

It can feel really tough to embrace ourselves.
To love those parts of us that feel unlovable.
This bit is okay, but if they knew about that bit... well...
We all did the best we could with what we had.
By facing our fears, and facing all of ourselves
We have the opportunity to love with our whole soul.

You are alright, exactly as you are.
There is no need to change or be different.
You can take off the mask you've been wearing.
I love you and your every experience and decision.
In amongst the confusion and uncertainty,
Together we can make sense of it all.

How do you feel about sitting with your emotions?
Which ones are more difficult to be with?
Who can support you to feel into your emotions?
What doesn't make sense at the moment?
Journal on this from different perspectives to see if
you can find a way for it to make more sense.
What if it had happened to a warrior?
What if it had happened to a king or queen?
What would a magician make of it?
What would love say?

You are Valuable

There is a sacred spark within you,
That is within each and every one of us.
It is valuable beyond any measure.
There is nothing you can ever say or do
to get rid of the spark.
It is there throughout your life.
It can never be hurt or damaged or broken.

It is always there, burning brightly,
Whether we can see it or not.
Every other person has the same spark
We are all valuable.
We are all important.
We are all sacred.

That includes you.
No matter what happens in your life
Or how things unfold – you are valuable.
No one can ever take it away from you.
By taking care of that spark
You'll see the miracles and magic that cross your path.

I'll help you to take care of that spark.
Looking after your mind, your body,
Your spirit and your soul.
When you feel connected with your spark
It inspires you to spread love everywhere you go.
Thank you for being you.

What helps you to connect with your sacred spark?
How do you show yourself you are valuable?
What would you do differently if you believed you were sacred?
Are babies valuable without having to do anything?
At what age do people stop being valuable?
What will you do regularly to connect with your value?

You have Shiny Ideas

We know we are loved.
We know we are safe.
We know we are valuable.
We are naturally creative and new ideas flourish.
Shiny ideas flow from you and I love to listen,
hearing the new possibilities you see.

You see things in a way no one else does.
Just like your unique finger print,
Your ideas come from a place
No one else can see.
It's really important you share them
As no one else can.

No one else has the same experience.
No one else has the same words.
This is your time.
This is your space.
Now is the time.
Speak your truth.

Sing it, play it, write it down.
Make a story out of it.
Paint it with your brightest paints.
Knit a scarf with the inspiration.
I am here alongside you, cheering you on
As your shiny ideas flow.

What shiny ideas do you have?
What shiny ideas would you have if no one was watching?
What lights you up?
How could you express these ideas?
What one thing will you do today to honour your shiny ideas?

You are Held

Whatever happens, you are held.
Whether you feel it or not, the holding is there.
I can hold you for as long as I can
With my earthly body
With my spirit,
And I am not the only one.

You are held by your friends, family,
By the people who live nearby.
We are all interconnected
Whether we notice it or not.
Yet we are held
Even more deeply than that.

Mother Earth is always here,
Holding our feet as we touch the ground.
She brings nourishing energy that flows upwards
Bringing nutrients and absorbing all the manure
we no longer need.
Taking the waste and using it to nourish the new seeds.
If you are still for a moment
You can feel your roots going deep down.
Find a tree that you can sit with and grow
your connection with Mother Earth.

Father Sky is vast, looking down on us,
bringing light energy
Down from the heavens, that flows through us
from our heads to our toes.
He is always there to hold you.
Give thanks to the sky, the moon, the sun and the stars
As ancient as the earth and as eternal in their energy.
You are always held.

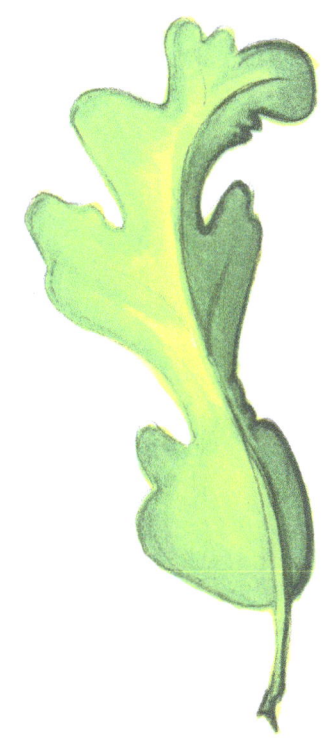

Find a tree that is near where you live that you can visit regularly.
Sit at the base of the tree, ideally where the trunk meets the ground.
Spend some time listening.
What do you hear?
What do you notice?
Repeat regularly.

You have Space

No matter how wild or wacky your ideas or thoughts are,
There is space for you.
The earth is huge, the sky is vast,
Space goes on and on forever.
You have all the space you need
To be yourself and bring your unique gifts to the world.

You have everything you need
To be the person you long to be.
I am here alongside you every step of the way.
There may be people who don't agree
Or who think your light shines too bright.
They are entitled to their opinions
No matter how wrong they are.

Don't let them stop you.
Don't shrink to make them happy.
Just shine your light
Somewhere else,
Where it is appreciated
And where you can flourish.

There is always room.
There is always space.
Find your allies.
Find the people who want to support you.
I am here alongside you with open arms
Wide enough to hold all the space you need.

What can you do less of to create some space?
What can you do less often?
What can you let go of?
Breathe a little deeper, creating space in your body
What does your mind need to let go of?

You are Loved

Throughout it all, you are loved.
Universal energy flows through us all
Nourishing us as it goes.
Universal energy is love,
You are loved by me, each and every day
From before you were born until after you die.

You are loved by your friends and family
and people nearby.
You are loved by Mother Earth
And Father Sky so deeply and eternally.
You can see evidence of this love
With every breath you take
That nourishes your body and soul.

You can feel it with every bite you eat
As the food nourishes you from the inside out.
You can feel it every time you shower or it rains
Water rinsing your body, cleansing it and refreshing it.
You can feel it in the warmth of the fire
And in the kiss of the breeze on your face.

You are loved by the earth and cherished
As the unique, sacred being you are.
Never doubt you are loved.
Feel it deep in your bones.
Sink into the nourishment of love
That is present in every moment.

What helps you remember you are loved?
What is good evidence as far as you are concerned?
Make reminders of this evidence and put it up
around your house so you always remember
you are loved.
Love is also an action – what can you do
to be more loving today?
Whatever you do,
remember you are lovable!

Step Three

Connecting with the universe

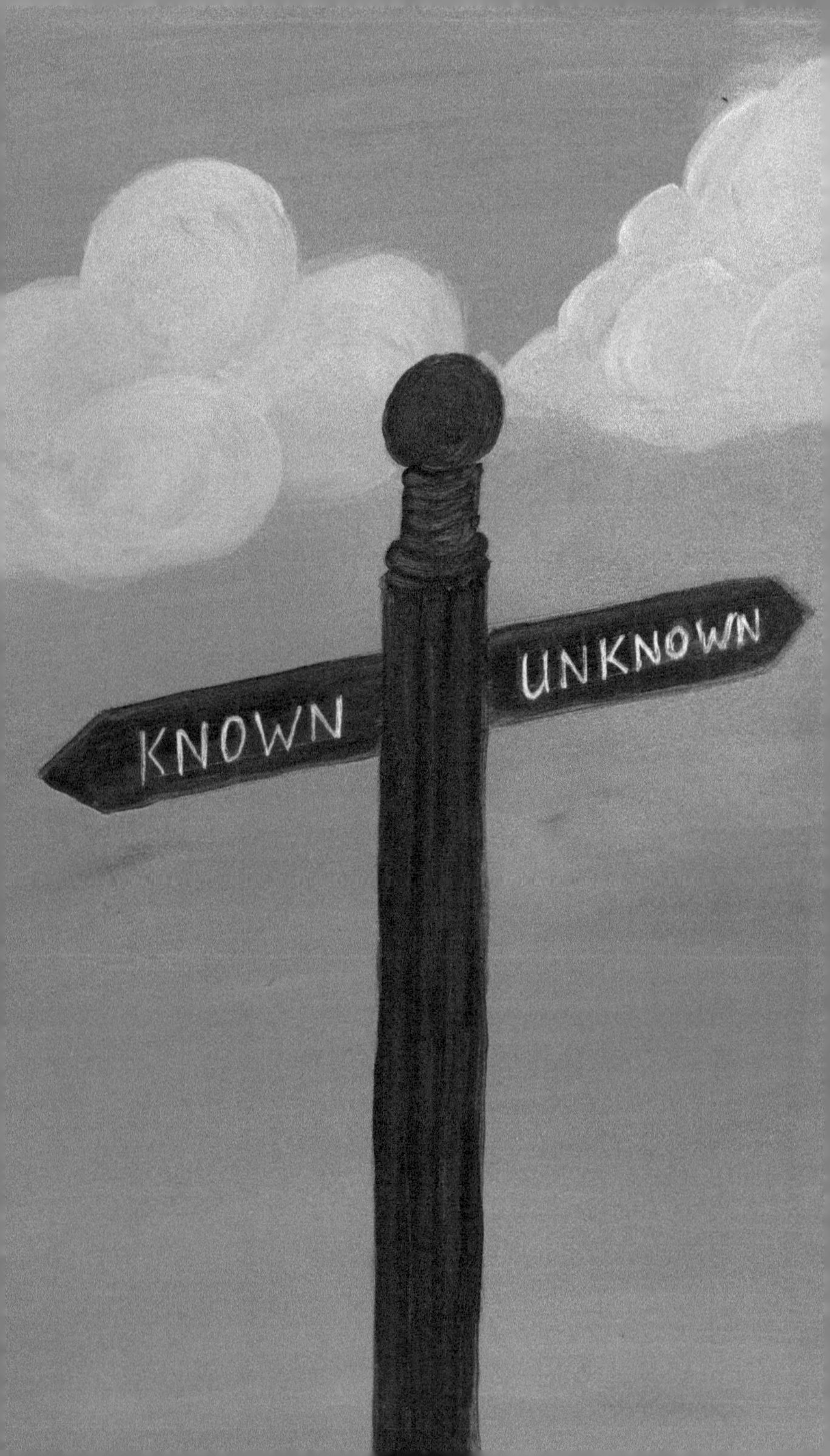
KNOWN
UNKNOWN

The Next Right Step

Which way do I turn?
What do I do next?
It is all so baffling.
I have no idea.
I feel paralysed with not knowing.
It feels like it should be obvious?

I take a deep breath.
I remember my connection with myself
and my inner child.
I put my hand on my heart
Appreciating that I am on my side.
I am not alone.
I am supported by one thousand hands.

Wise words calmly whisper to me
From some ancient place deep inside:
'You don't have to know all the details
Of the journey ahead of you.
You just have to take
The next right step.'

I look at my options.
Actually, the next small step feels clear
I might not know all the steps
But I can take the next step
That is right for me here and now.
I feel relief as I step.

What are you hoping to achieve at the moment?
What resources do you have to support you?
What are your options?
What one loving thing can you to today
that will be helpful?
If you are still not sure keep reading...

When I Don't Know

There are times when I still feel lost
I look at the options I can see
For the next step and they still
Don't feel right.
I'm connected with my heart
Yet the clarity doesn't land and I still feel uncertain.

The first thing I can do is nothing.
I can delay 'I need more time'
'I'll get back to you'
'I need more information'
'I'll think about that'
It is okay not to know.

The world keeps turning without my decision
The universe has its own timing and I surrender to that.
If there is still no clarity yet, I give space in other ways.
I take some time in nature,
I journal, I do some yoga.
I sit with the not knowing
and allow what's next to emerge.

When I least expect it, clarity pays me a visit.
Perhaps it is in a dream
Or when I am in the shower.
When my fear is not leading
The stars line up.
I'm ready and I know what I need to do.

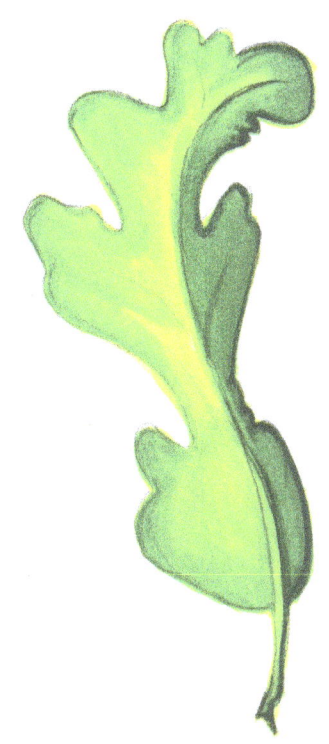

How can you give yourself more time?
How can you find out more information?
What creative ways could you explore it?
Perhaps try journalling, or drawing some options.
Do something different and write a poem about
the situation
What do you notice?

When Things Fall Apart

It felt so positive and yet
In a moment the world turns upside down,
I stumble and trip and land face down.
Shame burning my face as I wipe the dirt away.
How could this happen? I tried so hard.

The critical thoughts rush in,
It's all my fault, I didn't try hard enough
I failed and I just didn't see
It didn't work and it's all down to me.
I'm to blame, I'm the worst.
My inner critic won't give an inch.

I notice the stories I am telling myself
The echoes from the past, when I have punished myself.
Actually they are not true here and now
It's okay to try and for it not to work
I did my best and that is okay.
I'm still valuable even when things don't go to plan.

I rise up tall. I brush myself down.
My chest lifts as I breathe deeply.
I notice my feet on the ground.
I notice the flow of being in connection with myself
I can decide the next right step
It's okay to stumble and fall, learn and grow.

What stories do you regularly tell yourself?
What story would be more helpful?
Who else can help?
What helps you feel grounded and present?
Remember: It is all okay.

When I Fall Again

I've learned to allow myself one failure.
But two – surely that is too much to bear?
Somehow my inner critic is stronger this time
Fueled by the mistake.
This is the downfall.
This was the last chance and now it is all gone.

I'm amazed how quickly I can go back to the shadows.
As if the darkness has been waiting for me to trip up.
Ready to leap into action
When things get tough.
How can I rise again?
Where is the strength to pull myself up?

Yet the spark is still within me
It is refusing to go out.
I'm still breathing in and out
And while there is breath there is hope.
So I take my time to feel into it all,
Where I am wounded
and where I need to send myself love.

This time I pull the shawl around my shoulders
Warming me and feeling like a deep hug.
I have more awareness this time
Of what I need, what my body and soul need.
I reach out for what feels right,
Knowing I can shelter in my own loving kindness
as I heal.

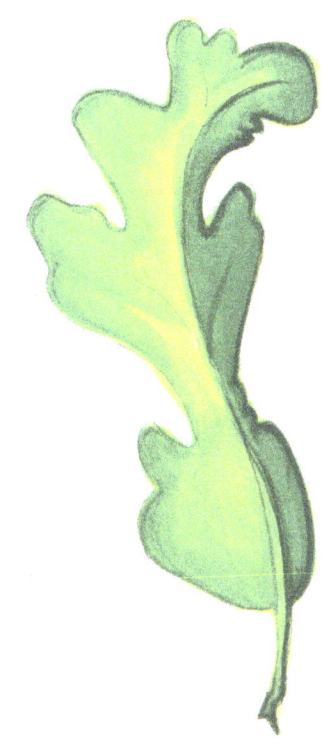

What helps you to believe in yourself?
When have you given something another go
and succeeded?
What if it was possible?
What if it was going to take 10 or 20
or 100 more tries?
You can do this –
  I believe in you.

Searching for the Light

I notice how the spark within me
Is growing stronger now.
The light from the sky is nourishing me,
While the energy from the earth is nourishing me,
I'm feeling more grounded and ready,
I'm connected with myself as I start to explore.

From this heartfelt place I can reach for the light.
I know the darkness is still there.
I know the shadows still exist.
Yet I am no longer afraid.
I know I have everything I need,
I can take the next right step that brings me home.

By welcoming the darkness and allowing it to be,
My journey is transformed.
I am here in the richness that is the flow of life.
While there is pain and fear
They are no longer in the driving seat
I am here and I welcome the light.

There is a beautiful balance to it all
Possibilities twinkle like stars
and opportunities are revealed.
There is a magic in the way life is unfolding.
I feel prickles down my back and my arms,
Feeling deeply I am doing what I need to do,
I can dare to dream.

What helps you to remember it is not all down to you?
Which of your ancestors' strength can you draw on?
If you had a magic wand, what would you wish for?
What else can you draw on?
Who else can help?
What if the universe really did have
your back?

Daring to Dream

Dreaming is a difficult thing to do
When I am triggered by my wounds.
If I'm anxious or scared or frozen,
My dreams can't emerge in panic.
They wait patiently for the gentle conditions
Where they flourish.

My path has connected me back with myself,
With loving support from the universe
I have brought myself home.
I have learned to trust, cherish and love myself.
Knowing the universal energy flows through me,
As I love everything that has gone before.

In this place where energy flows
Dreams start to whisper.
I notice them from the corner of my eye.
A flutter of excitement and possibility starts to dance
As if the universe is singing its ageless song
And I have finally made space to hear the melody.

Dreams flow through me
I am the vase and dreams pour in.
Light ones and fluffy ones,
Brightly coloured ones and gentle ones.
I tingle as I feel them flow
With such gratitude for the journey
That has brought me here.

When have you felt held and supported?
How has your appreciation for yourself grown?
What are you grateful for?
What do you dream of?
What would be even
more wonderful?

Co-creating with the Universe

Every step has been required to bring me to this place.
Every stumble and trip
All the doubt and shame, grief and anger.
The heartbreak, the desperation,
Has all been part of the richness
It feels clear it has all been required.
I welcome it with open arms, embracing all my journey.

Instead of my wounds leaking my lifeblood
They have become the source of my powerful medicine,
Deeply healing me.
I feel grounded with deep love for it all,
Appreciating every time I have been held and supported,
Knowing how many people have been alongside me.

I finally know where I start and where I end.
I understand what I can do with what I have.
There is power here
Co-creating with the universe,
Welcoming all that is and deciding my next right step,
For the highest good of all.

The wonder is awe-inspiring
The miracles are clear.
Every day is magical as I notice my part
in the bigger picture
I have everything I need
As I sink down into my body,
Taking my rightful place in the dance of life.

What do you still need to embrace?
What will help you to embrace it?
What is your powerful medicine?
How can you share that?
What else do you need?
Remember: You are love
in action! Enjoy!

About Charlie

Charlie has three incredible children who are a constant source of inspiration. They are lively, independent thinkers and each have their own unique way of being in the world. While life includes Autism, Down Syndrome and ADHD, there is so much joy, compassion and love.

Charlie has had plenty of opportunities to sit with her own huge range of emotions, and uses creative and healing approaches to help her to be the best mother she can be.

After a significant career as an Executive Coach, Charlie retrained in FreeMind Rapid Change Therapy, learning and creating tools for deep and lasting healing.

She is on a mission to inspire as many parents as possible to take their own healing journey.

She supports parents to become coaches, so they in turn can support and inspire other parents.

Access to Freemind Meditations

Charlie trained as a FreeMind Rapid Change Therapist with Tom Fortes Mayer because she found the FreeMind approach transformed her own life, and in the lives of those who took part in FreeMind training alongside her.

The FreeMind approach has brought a deep richness to Charlie's healing journey and has been part of the inspiration for this work.

FreeMind combines music therapy, sound frequency, sound healing and meditation tools to make the FreeMind experience more effective, enjoyable and engaging. However, it is the unique approach that transforms music into a healing metaphor, allowing people to discover everything they need within themselves. It is the ultimate self-healing approach.

Charlie regularly uses these meditations as part of her continuing healing. FreeMind's founder, Tom Fortes Mayer has kindly made a selection of these meditations available as his gift to you, to celebrate this book. This includes the full 70 minute inner child healing meditation. You can find these meditations and more about Tom's work here:
www.tomfortesmayer.com/resources

Thank You!

Thank you for using some of your precious life energy to read this book. You can find out more about support for your healing journey on a self-study basis, in a group with other parents on a similar journey and on a one to one basis with one of our qualified coaches at www.starseedparenting.org

My dream is for as many parents as possible with children who experience the world differently to have access to compassionate support when they need it.

Perhaps you'd like to find out about our funding scheme to support parents to become qualified coaches? So you can help other parents in similar situations?

Please visit our website for more information and do let other parents know they can start getting support today at: www.starseedparents.org

www.ingramcontent.com/pod-product-compliance
Lightning Source LLC
Chambersburg PA
CBHW061750070526
44585CB00025B/2851